Dad's Birthday

Written by Cynthia Rider,
based on the original characters
created by Roderick Hunt and Alex Brychta
Illustrated by Alex Brychta

OXFORD
UNIVERSITY PRESS

It was Dad's birthday.

Dad had a cake.

He had a bike.

Dad got on the bike.

"Go on, Dad," said Biff.

"Go on, Dad," said Chip.

"Go on, Dad," said Kipper.

Dad fell off!

Oh no!

Talk about the story

How did Dad make the children laugh when he was on the bike?

Why did Dad fall off the bike? Why isn't it a good idea to stand on a bike like that?

How do you think everyone felt when Floppy ran away with the cake?

Do you like going to parties? What is the best party you have been to?

Matching

Match the parcels to the presents.

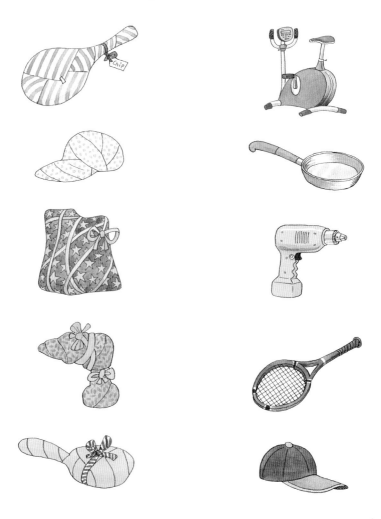